The Silver Lining in The Dark Cloud

Remilekun Jaiyeola

The Silver Lining in The Dark Cloud

A collection of short stories

Remilekun Jaiyeola

Dedication

This book is dedicated to God, my family, and everyone who has shaped my life and creative process over the years.

New Touch Int. Ltd 1A Pemberton Road,
Bradford, United Kingdom
+44-78-2385-2233
newtouchint_ltd@yahoo.com

TABLE OF CONTENTS

INTRODUCTION

The collection of short stories, 'The silver lining in the dark cloud' highlights various challenges people face in their journey of life, but which later end in joy.

'A Blessing in disguise' which is the first story in this book is about zeal and passion for success in Atiba village. The pupils took up the courage to work hard in putting an end to the problems the community was facing for so many years.

In 'Mixed Blessing', the second story in the collection, a barren woman sought God and He answered her prayers. She received immense support from her parents and husband. But was her mother-in-law supportive?

'Grace' tells a story of a sickle cell carrier who lost her job because of her condition. She well became single in a twinkle of an eye. Was she able to move on with her life? Was she able to find love?

Find out in these stories

A BLESSING IN DISGUISE

CHAPTER ONE

HARDSHIP ON THE SPOT

Atiba village slept in the burrow on the outskirts of Ibadan. A picturesque village predominantly populated by peasants. As usual, the street was deserted, and houses looked old. The shops along the road were few and the only school in that village is Best Legacy Government School. Just a few yards off the road, a borehole constructed by the well-known philanthropist who has been one of the few blessings to the village was filled with both old and young trying to fetch water for themselves, people as always impatient as they could be, are already arguing about who to fetch water next.

At the end of the road, a church and mosque stood meters away. Behind the mosque are some houses that looked decent enough - only those who have rich and well-to-do children could live in such kinds of buildings.

The government seem to have forgotten the Atiba village as all the efforts of the elders to seek their attention has proved abortive. They don't have electricity in their homes, the roads are bad, and with just a primary school and secondary school, the village is what we can call an undeveloped area.

Best Legacy Government School has about 200 pupils in total in various classes ranging from primary one to primary six. One could hear their voices as they chorused after their class teachers while taking their classes. Teachers have been discouraged to go on with their work since they have been underpaid. In fact, they are already being owed salary for 3 months, and the expected payment date is not even known. Despite this, teachers have decided to teach the students irrespective of the lack of receipt of their salaries. Most of these teachers are indigenes of Atiba Village and they all barely manage to survive by practising subsistence farming. Their focus is to help the children become better citizens in the future who will contribute their quota to the development of the village just as they are doing now.

Mr Obi the school Principal drove his old beetle car out of the school premises into the driveway slowly and acknowledged the villagers' greetings as he drove out. He drove to his house to meet his lovely wife at home.

Mrs Obi has been busy in the kitchen preparing a sumptuous meal for her husband - fufu and egusi soup filled with bush meat and ponmo. Mrs Obi has been dancing and rejoicing in the kitchen because she is eager to share the happy news with her husband.

The joy of every woman after getting married is to get pregnant and bear children. "Oh Lord I am very grateful" was the song she was singing all along and she didn't know when her husband entered the kitchen.

"My dear, I have been perceiving the aroma of your soup since I stepped into the house. Woah! I can see that you are

very happy. What is going on?" Mr Obi asked as he moved toward his wife to give her a warm hug.
"Welcome back my husband. It's the Lord's doing for us to be happy". Yeah! I have good news for you, but you must have your food before I share the news with you." She replied.
"Must I finish eating before you'll tell me about the good news? that will take a long time knowing that I eat slowly." Won't you tell me now before I die of apprehension? He begged.
"Yes, trust me the good news will make you happy for the rest of your life. Just calm down, go and freshen up while I set the table for you." She said.

*******After about 20 minutes************

"This food is very delicious; I am so happy I married a chef." Mr Obi said as he was busy enjoying the meal with his wife.
"I am so happy you are enjoying your meal darling. I decided to make this meal a special one for you. You deserve it, my husband." She said as she winked at him.
"Wait ooo. Hope it's not that you need more money, and you decided to use this delicious food to bribe me? Remember we have not been paid for a while now" He asked.
"Not at all my husband. I know you've not gotten your salary for the last three months, and the farm has been helping to sustain our family so far. The good news I have is that I'm pregnant." She said happily.
"Wait, did I hear you say you are pregnant? Ehh-- heh. Jesus, you are good." He shouted for joy.

He and his wife danced for thirty minutes to thank God for his mercies over their lives and for remembering them with this expected baby, singing different songs and smiling together.

“Woah, my dear, I am the happiest man on earth. So, I am going to be a father soonest? I am excited. Let me go and check the trap on the farm. I must make delicious pepper soup for you.” He said.

“Thank you, my husband. You deserve the best. I appreciate you.” She said.

The following morning, Mr Obi woke up early to do the house chores for his dear wife because he doesn't want her to stress herself. He decided to make her favourite food alongside the bush meat he got from the trap set on the farm the previous day. He woke his wife up to instruct her not to go out for the rest of the day but just to have her bath, eat and sleep so as not to stress herself.

Mrs Obi was surprised to see what her husband has done for her – he has done the early morning chores and prepared meals that his wife will eat for the whole day - and she thanked him as he left home for school at 7:00 am.

“I think it's better to be getting pregnant every year so that my husband can be taking care of me every day,” she said aloud.

CHAPTER TWO

RESPONSIBILITY OF A LEADER

Back to Best Legacy Government School. Children were running towards the school gate to ensure they meet up before the assembly starts as the principal has always frowned at late coming and reprimanded latecomers.

At exactly eight o'clock, the timekeeper rang the bell for the commencement of the assembly. As usual, all pupils and teachers trooped out of the classrooms and staffroom respectively to the assembly ground. The morning procession was done as usual. Teachers went around to inspect the pupils to make sure that they are clean as Mr Obi came forward to give his speech.

“Good morning children.” He said.

“Good morning Sir.” They chorused.

“As we all know that your education has been going on well in this school despite your teachers not being remunerated as expected, I would like to urge you all to take your academics seriously and make the best use of this opportunity. I would like to encourage you all to be good ambassadors of this school anywhere you find yourselves. Also, I want you to remember that your teachers are here to mentor and listen to you anytime you desire. We will continue to try our best in whatever circumstances.” He said with confidence.

The children clapped after his speech and went to their various classes.

Mrs Chike, a plump, fair complexion woman walked out of the

staffroom, heading towards the primary six class to teach the pupils social studies.
She entered majestically in high spirit to teach the students.
“Good morning class how are you today?” She asked.
“Good morning ma, we are fine, thank you.” They replied.
Today I'll be teaching on the topic “Responsibilities”.
According to the Father of Social studies, Responsibility is a state of having to deal with something or having control over someone. What this means is that responsibility allows us to take ownership of something, a situation, or a position.
“Do you understand class?" Mrs Chike asked.
“Yes ma”. They chorused.
“Okay, so let's continue”. She said.
“Reasons to be responsible: It is the foundation of your success; it puts you in control of your life, it is a sign of maturity and makes you ready for action. If you are responsible, then you will be seen as reliable and trustworthy by others. You will become a person of excellence who exceeds expectations”. She explained to the pupils. After the forty minutes lesson taught by Mrs Chike, some of her pupils went ahead to ask questions to which she responded.
The following week, the principal and other teachers decided to elect prefects from the primary six class to take over some responsibilities and help them develop leadership skills.
In the staff room, all teachers were in their seats before the principal’s arrival so as not to be scolded for coming late.
The principal was accompanied by the Vice Principal into the staff room. All the teachers stood up to welcome them.

“Good afternoon Sir.” They all chorused

“Good afternoon everybody”. He answered quickly.

“Our time is far spent, and I don't want to take much of our time any further. I want us to nominate the best pupils as prefects for the leadership positions in the school for the current academic session. I want them to have that leadership spirit so that later in future they will be able to help their community wherever they find themselves”. He demanded.

Mrs Chike raised her hand to comment. " You are right Sir, I taught them last week about responsibilities and it is high time they started putting all they have learnt into practice.

I'll nominate Ezekiel as the head prefect boy and Grace as the head prefect girl. Those two nominees have been taking part in inter-community competitions so far and bringing the victory home. Asides from being brilliant, I have also noticed they are always willing to help their mates and younger children in their studies. I am convinced they will do well in these positions.

Everyone agreed with what Mrs Chike said and some other pupils too were nominated for social, health, timekeeper, and punctuality perfect positions.

Since we have all chosen the best candidates for the various prefect positions, Mrs Chike is to prepare all the primary six pupils for a special assembly next week Monday. It's going to be a surprise to all the pupils on the assembly ground that day. Just ensure you tell them all to dress well. Mr Obi instructed.

“Yes, Sir, I'll do just that”. She answered.

All the pupils have been given the news that some prefects will be selected to take up some responsibilities in the school. The primary six pupils as instructed by Mrs Chike agreed to come top-notch to school on Monday as they are all eager to end the suspense of who will be appointed, so, they all decided to dress well per adventure they might be called.

As usual, Samuel rang the bell to signal a call for gathering at the assembly ground in the morning and all pupils were excited to rush to the assembly ground to hear the exciting news of those that will be nominated as the prefects of the school.

The assembly started with worship and praises to God almighty to thank Him for sparing their lives, then to sing the national anthem and pledge.

The principal came up to give his speech and announce the prefects to the pupils.

“Good morning children.” He shouted happily with a smile on his face.

“Good morning Sir.” They chorused.

“How are you this morning?” He asked.

“We are fine, thank you, sir.” They responded.

“I am very sure you all have been anticipating who the prefects will be. Just not to waste much of our time, I will start calling out their names.” He quickly said

"The head prefect boy will be Ezekiel Thompson while the head prefect girl will be Grace Adeleke." He announced.

Everyone clapped for joy admitting the surprise. Afterwards, everyone became silent as he continued to announce the names of other prefects, and then came more thunderous applause and hearty congratulations to them.

These students have demonstrated good habits and that is why our teachers have unanimously decided to assign them various leadership positions so they could be role models to the rest of you.

Congratulations once again to your prefects. Please ensure you continue to be characters worthy of emulation to the rest of these pupils. You have a lot on your plate, and I am sure, you are all capable of handling both your academics and your newly assigned roles effectively. I wish you all the best. He said.

The newly appointed head boy moved forward and thanked the principal and teachers for their trust in them to make a change and promise to carry out all assigned roles in the interest of all. Everyone was released to their various classes. Ezekiel the head prefect boy summoned the new prefects after school hours for a brief meeting before they could call it a day. He congratulated them once again for the achievement and encouraged them to do well during their tenure as the future holds better opportunities for them.

So, let's get down to business. As we all know, Atiba community has a lot of problems plaguing it, from poor electricity to bad roads, bad stalls in the market square to poor healthcare facilities, a few boreholes, and even bad structures in this our school. I want us to decide on how to help our school and the community at large. Please can you suggest how we can go about it?

"Hmmm, there are lots of problems in this our Atiba community. Have you even forgotten that our teachers have not been paid for the past three months? All they have been doing is just what we can call selfless service. Grace, the head prefect girl lamented."

"Some children have been discouraged to continue their education after primary six, and most female children end up getting married to older men due to poverty. The boys end up becoming slaves to the few rich people in this community or they end up becoming thugs for our politicians who don't even want to help our community in whatever way. All they know best is to squander public funds lavishly." Samuel the timekeeper lamented too.

How are we going to solve all these problems? they look like heavy mountains to us right now?" Paul the health prefect said.

"We don't even have good primary health care in this community and some people have died due to various sicknesses.", Sade said.

"We have all mentioned the problems we have been facing in this community and I think we can help the school and the community as a whole to solve the problems." Ezekiel unfolded the cardboard in his hands before he continued.

"With this strategy, I believe we would be able to solve these

problems." Ezekiel confidently said.
All the prefects agreed to the roadmap shared by Ezekiel from his cardboard, and they promised to work as a team towards helping the community.

So, we will meet with the principal tomorrow after school hours to brief him on our plan and resolutions. Thank you all for showing up, I appreciate it. Ezekiel said.
The following day, the prefects met with the school principal, Mr Obi to brief him about their plans and seek advice on how to go about it. Mr Obi was impressed by their plans and decided to help. At least, the prospect of a miracle is worth a trial. Part of the plans was to see the village head and seek his support on how to reach out to the Governor of the state to plea for immediate attention.
As planned, as early, as ten o'clock, they assembled at the village head's house to see him. One of the guards ushered them to the garden to wait for the village head.
"Please hold on, the Chief will soon be here." He said.
Fifteen minutes later, the King entered the garden. Mr Obi and the prefects bowed to show him respect as he entered.
Welcome my people and I am sorry for keeping you waiting, I was attending to something in the palace, and it took much of my time. The Chief pleaded as we moved towards his throne to sit.
"To what do I owe this visit." He asked.

We are here because of the situation in our community, and we want you to help us reach out to the Governor. We believe that with your influence, he will be able to help us, and our lives will be better. Mr Obi begged.

The chief shrugged and said "Well, I have reached out to the Governor several times but all my pleas for him to help us has proved abortive. I have sent several letters to him with no positive response whatsoever. The Governor also complained of a lean budget and monthly allocation from the Federal Government"

"But I heard there is a spelling competition coming up in the city and that the winner of the competition will be the Governor of the state for a day. This means that irrespective of gender, the person will be able to sign contracts, make a wish or just accomplish some assignments. All will happen just in one day. Can we get anyone to represent the Atiba community in the competition? I think that will go a long way in helping us or what do you think?". The Chief asked.

The prefects could not hide their joy as to the good news they heard and immediately asked the Chief when the competition would take place. The Chief affirmed, "The competition will hold in 2 months and I think there is enough time for you to prepare and make this community proud.

"I will represent the school," Ezekiel said.

"I will be the one to represent the school," Samuel shouted.

"I must be the one to represent the school," Grace shouted with enthusiasm written all over her face.

“Silence. Do you children realize we are in the presence of the Chief? where are your manners? Don’t argue on this matter.” Mr Obi resolved.

“Your performances in the next few weeks will determine who is going to represent the school in the competition. Now, apologize to the Chief for such rude behaviour.” He instructed.

“We are very sorry Sir; we apologize Sir.” They pleaded.

The Chief could not help but laugh and accepted the children’s apologies. He shrugged and said, “Well, I love your disposition and confidence to act and represent your school. I am so proud of you all and I will give you all the support needed to participate in the competition. Keep it up.”

CHAPTER THREE

THE TIMELY PREPARATION

All hands were on deck at Best Legacy Government School. The perfects were preparing to take part in the spelling bee competition that will come up in the city. They believe it is an opportunity for them to win and solve the lingering community problems.

The principal walked into primary six class to motivate and encourage the selected prefects to take part in the competition and work hard towards their goals. Five prefects were selected to practice for the competition but two of them will make the final duo to represent the school in the competition.

Ezekiel, Grace, Samuel, Peter, and Gloria were selected by their teacher, Mrs Chike based on their performances in English so far. During school break, Mrs Chike called them to her office to give them new words to learn and find new words in the dictionary.

“How are you all doing today?” She asked.

“We are fine Ma.” They answered.

“So, let's get down to business. I have written some words for you to practice in this book.” She said.

“You'll write them in your spelling book and learn them at home. Let me ask you some and let's see how prepared you are.”

“Ezekiel, spell the word, Encyclopedia.” She instructed.

“Okay, ma. E-n-c-y-c-l-o-p-e-d-i-a.” He answered.

“Good, that's very correct. Well done my boy.” She commended

“Grace, spell the word, hippopotamus.” She instructed.

“H-i-p-p-o-p-o-t-a-m-u-s.” She answered confidently.

“Good, well done, you guys are making me proud already.” She commended.

She was very happy with them all seeing their preparedness for the competition. She motivated them to continue to practice till the day of the competition. She also ensured she groomed the pupils for the competition by meeting with them twice a week to sharpen them up. The practice continued for weeks, and all hands were on deck, geared to ensure success. The pupils didn't hesitate to help each other in learning. It has been announced by the principal that the best two participants out of a total of five will be selected to represent Best Legacy Government School in the upcoming spelling bee competition.

**********A week to the competition**********

After school hours Mr Obi was happy to go home to meet his pregnant wife. He got bush meat from the farm to prepare for his wife as he knows it is her favourite, especially since being pregnant. He had ensured his wife was well taken care of and he doesn't allow her to stress herself since it was her first time of conception since their marriage of 8 years.

“Welcome my husband, how was school today?” She asked

happily as she moved towards him to hug him.

"Thank you, my dear, school is fine. I've missed you so much." He answered while he hugged her too.

"I hope you didn't stress yourself today and I hope you're very fine. Were you able to eat the meal I prepared for you in the morning?" He questioned.

"My husband, how many questions do you want me to answer at the same time." She queried.

"Don't mind me. I am just after your welfare. You know you mean a lot to me." He answered. "I am fine dear; you don't need to worry too much." She replied.

"My dear, as usual, I got bush meat from the farm, a very big one at that. I will have to go to the kitchen to prepare it for you. Just allow me to change my clothes and I'll prepare them immediately. I will see to it that you get the best attention from me before you give birth and be the best father to our child too. You and my child must be very healthy." Mr Obi's voice sounded tired.

After that, he prepared the pepper soup for his pregnant wife to eat. They had time to discuss as couples and went to sleep. The following day was Saturday, and the room was pitch-dark except for the single ray of light that shone into the house. Mrs Obi felt a sharp pain in her stomach. She was shocked at the excruciating pain. "Yeah-eh! Ah-ah-G-o-d". She screamed. She broke out in a sweat. Blood was coming out of her body. She was crying and weeping uncontrollably.

Mr Obi entered the room to see his wife weeping

uncontrollably. He dropped the tray of food in his hands on the table to help his wife. He was surprised at the turn of the event. He knew how well he had taken care of his pregnant wife and not allowed her to stress herself. He felt very sad but decided not to show it to his wife. He drove the car in a rush to the primary health care centre for his wife to get proper treatment. Unlike many other times, thankfully, a doctor was around to take care of her. After the care, the doctor called him to his office to break the sad news of the loss of the baby to Mr Obi and encouraged him to hope for a better one next time.

He entered the small room to see his wife. The smell of the hospital took over the whole place.

My wife, all will be well. I know it is well with our souls. Why are you thinking? Mr Obi sat down. She did not answer.

“Why won't I think? I was careful not to stress myself and you were more than helpful through it all, so what should warrant losing my three months pregnancy,” she accused.

Look, my dear, I believe God is going to bless us with plenty of children. This is not the end of the world, besides the doctor said you are medically fit and good to go. My wife, please you don't have to worry yourself. It is well."

“Don't wife me, just leave me alone. Leave me alone, she snapped her eyes in a flash of fury.

“Oh, Sandra, please. I know you are very sad right now and you don't feel like doing anything or talking to me. Please calm

down."
Mrs Obi stared unseeingly into space. She bit her lower lip and tried to repress her grouchy feelings.

"Sandra, talk to me, please don't keep mute. Come on, where is the virtuous character in you? I will surely make it up to you. I will do everything as a man to ensure you do not feel sad and to ensure we are back on track. All I am always after is your welfare remember?

Seeing that he got no response from Sandra his wife, he began to mumble like a baby. He did it for like thirteen minutes just to cheer her up and as much as Sandra tried, she couldn't help but laugh despite the sadness and the anger.

With laughter on her lips, she tapped her husband on the shoulder to approve of all the words of encouragement he gave to her.

It is all right, my husband. I will not worry myself any longer, we will keep trying. God will bless our effort."

They both laughed and left for their home after the doctor discharged her to go home.

The day of the competition came, and Best Legacy Government School was ready to compete with other schools in the city. All preparations have been done. Ezekiel and Grace were selected based on merit to represent their school. The Chief of the community volunteered to take the pupils to the city in his official car for the competition. He ensured he provided everything they needed for their success.

Best Legacy competed with various schools both public and

private in the city. It was a fiercely contested competition. At one point, all hope was lost as Ezekiel missed out on the spelling of the word "Kwashiorkor", only for the other schools too to miss their turn of spelling. Finally, it came to only two schools after 4 hours and several rounds of spelling. Even the Chief could not stand the tension he felt watching the contestants that he had to go seat in his car to listen from his radio as it was broadcast live on all radio stations in the State. The Chief kept praying that these children from Best Legacy School wins. After the duo of Ezekiel and Grace had spelt all words assigned to them, the other school, Foremost International School missed their spelling of the word "Pseudonym". To confirm Best Legacy School as the winner, they needed to spell the word and Grace graciously took to the podium to spell it correctly! What a day it was as Mr Obi and Mrs Chike jumped off their seats to hug each other and shed tears of joy. It was a great victory for the school. The Chief, Mr. Obi, Mrs Chike, and the whole community were so happy. Victory at a last.

Everyone in the community screamed for joy after watching and listening to Ezekiel and Grace on the television and radio. Their courageous attitude melted the hearts of the community members, both old and young and attracted Atiba village to people outside the community. Children who have stopped going to school were already having a change of mind to get enrolled back in school.

The state Governor who was also delighted to see a school in a remote village show academic prowess could not hide his emotions as he mounted the podium. Over to the winners, what is your wish and what do you want to do for your society? The Governor asked as he conferred the title of "Governor for a day" on Ezekiel. The audience clapped for Ezekiel and Grace as they moved to the podium.

Our village, Atiba, has a lot of problems on the ground that we want to be solved and actions must start immediately.

I, Ezekiel, representing Best Legacy Government School, Atiba and as Governor for today hereby order that electricity should be fixed in the community, teachers' salaries should be paid without delay, and primary health care centres should be renovated as well as the bad roads fixed.

"Grace, do you have anything to add to what I have said so far?" He asked as he turned towards her. "Yes, I have." She replied.

In addition to what he had said. Free medical care should be given to both old and young in the community, employment opportunities should be given to scholars like us after we finish primary school. Thank you.

The Governor was surprised to have listened to the pupils'

wishes as they didn't ask for money for themselves but requested opportunities just for the betterment of the community. In awe at their compassionate heart, he opted to offer them money, as well commencing work on what the children had requested. He also apologized for not yielding positively to the letters written by the Chief on grounds of lean allocation from the Federal Government and commended the Chief and the teachers that came along with them for bringing them up well.

Mr Obi and the teachers were so happy at the positive change effected by the request of Ezekiel and Grace after winning the competition. The teachers were more than motivated to teach the children more and some of the children who had stopped attending school were encouraged to return to school. Some two months afterwards, Mrs Obi got pregnant again and Mr Obi as usual was more than pleased to pamper his wife. After another seven months, Mr and Mrs Obi welcomed a set of triplets into their home, a boy and two girls, bringing an end to childlessness in their family.

All that happened in Atiba village ended as a blessing in disguise.

MIXED BLESSINGS

CHAPTER ONE

THE DASHING HOPE

"Wake up, sleepy head. Or are you planning to sleep all day?" Dotun stroked Funmi's hair gently. She made no move while her face looked calm with a beautiful smile. Her breathing was even.

"Funmi, won't you get up? Do you think I have the whole day to play around? I have a conference meeting with the master contractor today and if I am not mistaken, I suppose you have a business meeting with one of your clients today too." Dotun tried to be firm.

Funmi kept on smiling; eyes closed. Dotun grabbed the duvet from her, revealing her pink nightgown, her long chubby legs, and the freshness of her body. She rolled over on her side, still smiling.

Dotun was irked. He threw up his hands in submission.

"Look, woman, if your business doesn't mean much to you, mine does and I have got to keep it to remain relevant in this family, if not for your sake, then for the sake of our unborn child. Now, will you get up and make breakfast, or do I kiss the daylight out of you!"

"Now you're talking," Funmi said, opening one eye and couldn't help but laugh at her husband. "You see, this is still like a dream to me." She closed her eyes and decided to sleep again.

Dotun shook his head in amazement. He had to relinquish the fact that his wife needed some modicum of comfort, and he shook her less gently than expected.

"Well, if a marriage of six months still looks like a dream to you, then may God help us ooo." He said sarcastically.

"Anyways, as I said earlier, I need some breakfast."

"Steady, darling. We are going out together, aren't we?"

"If you go on making a fool out of me this morning, I guess I will have to go without my beautiful wife. I'm sure you can find your way."

"Babe don't be crossed with me. I was only joking, what's the harm in that? Or can't I play with my husband anymore? Anyway, good morning," she greeted, sitting up in the bed. "Don't mind my grogginess darling," said Funmi.

"Morning, sweetheart. But I didn't sound crossed, or did I? Did you sleep well? How is our baby?" he asked patting her belly and stroking her hair at the same time.

"Our baby is fine. So how is my husband this morning?" Funmi cast a look of admiration and affection.

"I will be fine if my wife gives me a hug," he replied in a chubby voice.

Funmi gave him a warm hug that seemed to turn the atmosphere into a heavenly paradise leading to the couple giggling in laughter like children watching their favourite cartoon.

The phone rang, cutting the scene short. “Blast!” Dotun hissed. “If it's possible I'd have that phone switched off. It rings at the most unexpected time.” With a wicked wink, he got up from the bed.

Funmi quickly tidied up the room and went straight to the bathroom to run a bath for Dotun while she retired to the kitchen to make his favourite breakfast of custard and pancakes. She sang melodious songs as she was cooking.

“This breakfast is very delicious. I love it. Thank you so much, dear. I appreciate.” Dotun said as he patted his wife's head.

“You are welcome. Anything just to make my husband happy.” She chuckled.

After their breakfast. They all set out for the work of the day. Funmi went for her business meeting and Dotun also attended the conference meeting. Dotun ensured he called his wife during the day to know about her welfare. She complained of feeling dizzy and tired and Dotun ensured she left her meeting early to go home to rest, assuring her he would get some fruits for her on his way home.

The driver drove the Toyota car into the driveway. Funmi nodded to respond to the security man's greeting as she walked into the house - a duplex that can house a family of ten. The inside was painted in the same colour as the outside, butter, and cream colour. The duplex consisted of two sitting rooms, five big bedrooms, a kitchen, three toilets with a bathtub attached, and a store. The kitchen led into the well-kept garden. The living room is adorncd with homey and beautiful pictures. The furnishing was gorgeously done to denote the house of a rich man with pieces of artwork lining the walls of the ventilated room.

Funmi threw her bag on the table and pulled off her shoes as she walked toward the bedroom. She gently removed her clothes and pulled a long green cotton tee shirt over her head while she went straight to the kitchen to make fresh juice from the fridge. She brought out a little cold smoothie, uncapped it, and drank the whole content, then headed straight to her room to sleep.

Her husband came in some hours later to meet her sleeping and decided not to disturb her remembering she complained of dizziness earlier in the day. He thought she needed rest and the pregnancy is already taking the best of her.

The following day, Funmi went to the hospital for her antenatal care. As she entered the reception of the hospital, she hummed to herself as she walked. A frown creased her brow as a tinge of pain went through her, narrowing in a flash. She shouted due to the pain. Immediately, she couldn't walk again, and blood was coming out of her body already.

Someone on his way out saw her and helped beckon people

seated in the reception to hurriedly get the nurse's attention. Funmi found it difficult to believe what just happened to her in the space of a few minutes at the hospital. She couldn't just come to terms with it after waiting for two years just to be able to get pregnant. The Doctor quickly came around to attend to her since it was an emergency. After stabilizing her, he had no choice other than to call her husband on the phone being that he's their family doctor.

****

I feel like seeing Funmi," Mrs Adebire voiced her emotions as she set the dining table.
"Go on," her husband responded. "This is the third time you have said the same thing in the past two days." He said
"I wish I could just see her this very moment, I wish she had not gotten married yet" Mrs Adebire complained further. She took a seat beside her husband after setting the food on the dining table.
"Oh, my dear child!" She stared at her husband just to get his attention, but he continued scrolling the pictures on his phone.
"I have called to check up on her to know how she and the baby are faring, but I feel like seeing her face to face. Mrs Adebire held her head in her palm and closed her eyes momentarily. Still, Mr Adebire paid no notice.

"Femi, don't you miss your daughter, aren't you even bothered about how Funmi is coping? Doesn't it even bother you how she will be feeling right now?" Mrs Adebire demanded, assessing his countenance.

He was so busy with his phone. No answer was forthcoming. Angrily she hit the table and caught the attention of her husband. He looked up at her with an expressionless countenance.

"I was talking to you," she blurted out. Is that why you hit the table with such discourteousness? What were you saying?" He asked.

"What was I saying? It's all right for you to be so indifferent to all these. Not that I expected concern from you anyway. But at least, courtesy demands that you respond to my concerns, and the last time I checked, she is our only daughter and child." Mrs Adebire fumed.

Femi raised his hands to refrain her from talking further. "Many thanks to our mother in Israel, for the fatherly right you have admitted.

I just don't see us doing ourselves any good worrying about Funmi, remember, worry does no good." God is in control".

"Hun-un. Do you mean there is nothing to worry about? What if her condition is making her sick? What if she's not having an appetite for food? What if she doesn't feel agile to do anything for herself? First-time pregnancy can be tiring?" She shouted.

"Look, don't get unduly anxious, our daughter is fine. Besides,

Dotun is with her." Femi cautioned.
"Please let's eat, before it gets cold." He added.

* Back to the hospital******************

The doctor decided to put a call through to Dotun. He called Dotun's office from the hospital. The shrill ringing of the telephone cut into his daydreaming. He stretched his hands towards the receiver and lifted it off the hook.
"Hello, this is Doctor James."
"Ah, Doctor, how have you been? What came up?" Dotun asked
After asking about his work and if he was disposed to speak, he continued. Funmi was at the hospital earlier for her antenatal care and while making her way into the reception, she had excruciating pain and by the time we examined her, we discovered she suffered a miscarriage.
"What did you just say, Doctor?"
"I am sorry for the loss, but you need to be strong for your wife"
"How is she now, where is my wife at the moment?" asked Dotun
"She is resting. In a couple of hours, she should be awake." Said the Doctor
"I'll be right over." Said Dotun
Dotun dropped the receiver and reached for his car keys in a rush to head for the hospital.

CHAPTER TWO

THE LONG WAITING

Three years later, Funmi and Dotun were still trusting God for another child. All efforts in getting pregnant again proved abortive. This had made Funmi devastated and tired of life due to the nagging and complaints from her mother-in-law. Every call from her is based on questioning Funmi about when she will give her grandchildren.

Dotun had consistently frowned at this insensitivity from his mother and tried all his best to talk senses into her to be patient with them as they have been trying all within the medical field to get pregnant again. His mum has even gone as far as advising Dotun to marry another lady from the village since his wife has just suddenly become a barren woman who is just eating all the food in the house without producing fruits.

The sharp ringing of the bell cut Funmi's reverie. She got up and called out. "Just a minute."

She went to the bedroom to get her housecoat. She feels tired even though it was still too early for that.

As she opened the door, a stream of sunshine gushed in. She blinked as the sharp illumination teased her eyes. She looked up into her mother-in-law's eyes in surprise but with welcoming smiles. Funmi was scared as her mother-in-law was the last person expected at her doorstep at this time. She doesn't want to see her mother-in-law, not until she can give birth to a child .

Good morning ma," she called out weakly...

"What is good in the morning? Funmi, what is good, when you have not given me my grandchildren? Do you want me to go to my grave without seeing my grandchildren?" She exclaimed as she walked in, closing the door after her.

"You even look pale! Are you ill?"

Funmi sat down. She did not answer.

"How will you even be able to give birth to my children when you look this pale? You have eaten all the food in the house, and yet, find it difficult to get pregnant after the one-time miscarriage you had." She mocked.

Funmi started endearingly into space. She bit her lower lip and tries to repress her feelings.

"See, young lady! I give you just three months to get pregnant for my son, otherwise, I will make sure he impregnates another lady outside. I can't withstand all of this. What is your value in this house when there are no kids at home? Nothing like mummy welcome back, or grandma when next are you coming to visit us?" She sarcastically demonstrated.

After all her nagging and mockery, she finally left, asking Funmi to let Dotun know all that she threatened at his return. As soon as she left, Funmi soaked in tears ran into the bedroom to call on God to intervene in her matter. The stress she had gone through was just too much for her to bear. She was in deep thought in her bedroom, and she didn't even know when her husband entered.

"Funmi, what happened to you?" Dotun exclaimed as he

walked in, closing the door after him. “You look perturbed! My mum came to disturb you right?”

“Look Funmi, I know you must be very mad at her but whilst it’s disturbing to think about how you must have been harassed, could you please forgive her misgivings because of me?”

“Funmi, I know you feel very sad about the matter but as far as I am concerned, you aren’t a barren woman, and we are in this cockpit together. You will bear fruits to everyone’s surprise. I trust the God we serve to do it in His time. It is never too late for God to turn our sorrows into joy and laughter.” Funmi, just look at my face.

He decided to cuddle her and make her laugh. He did this for a while till she couldn’t help but laugh despite her sadness. With laughter in her voice, she said “thanks for having my back dear”.

Funmi smiled at Dotun’s show of concern and compassion. He had a look of admiration on his face, and something else, which he tried to hide – pity for the plight his wife must have been through. Funmi always found it difficult to get sad whenever her husband is around because he will surely find ways to make her happy irrespective of whatever they may be passing through.

“Have you eaten this afternoon?” He asked, fondling her ears.

“Hmm, I have not eaten anything this afternoon, besides you met me lost in thought when you came in.”

Let me get into the kitchen and find something sumptuous for you to eat,” Give me some minutes,” Dotun affirmed.

She watched as he walked towards the kitchen with masculine grace. She closed her eyes and allowed the warmth of the room to envelop her. Funmi listened to the click clank that came from the kitchen. At this time, she cared less about the present state of not having children but reminisced about the reassurances she got from Dotun when situations like this occur. Simply put, Dotun remained the second foot on which her world stood and that was all that mattered.

The rest of the day was a welcoming change for her as she was comforted in the word of God. After their lunch, she and her husband had time to commune with God through the reading of their bible and prayers.

"My dear, let's check the bible to hear from God." He said as he checked for his bible at the table beside the sofa.

"No problem dear, I need strength to overcome this storm." She affirmed.

He opened his bible to read. According to 1 Samuel 2:1-2 "And Hannah prayed and said: My heart rejoices in the Lord; My horn is exalted in the Lord. I smile at my enemies because I rejoice in Your salvation. No one is holy like the Lord, for there is none besides You, nor is there any rock like our God." He read out aloud to her hearing.

"Hmmm, will God answer my prayers too?" She asked amidst her tears.

"Hannah prayed and God acknowledged her prayers. He gave

her Samuel that became useful in God’s hands. She cast her problems before God, poured out her mind to God and at the end, the Lord turned her sadness into joy.” He counselled.

“But I am very weak to pray. I have lost hope in God actually. Together with your mum’s nagging and mockery, I am tired of life. The only thing that hasn’t made me leave this marriage or committed suicide is just because of you and my parents. But truth be told, I am tired of waiting.” She lamented.

“Ah, please my dear, don’t do anything stupid. God will answer our prayers. We need to increase our intercession and supplication to God. It’s better late than never and as we know; God is too faithful to fail. There have been countless people both in the bible and on this earth with resounding testimonies of how God came through for them amid severe crises like this. One thing is sure, He will surely do it for us. The word of God never changes, and God will cause everything to work in our favour.” He encouraged.

“I believe God will do it for me too. I trust in his word.” She affirmed happily.

That’s the spirit I love to see my dear. God has done it already and he is too faithful to fail us. He enlightened.

Come on, stand up my dear and let’s start praying to God. He said.

Let’s start with praises. Let’s listen and dance to Nathaniel Bassey’s song. Then we pray afterwards.

They worshipped and prayed to God for two hours and were relieved of the burden of childlessness. They were both happy and thanked God immensely afterwards.

CHAPTER THREE

GLORY DAWN

Funmi sprawled on the couch supporting her head with her arms. She smiled to herself like a baby.

A firm and persistent knock roused her. As she scrambled up and walked to the door, she unlocked the door to open it, wondering who the caller was.

"Mother!" She screamed," and Father too!" She hugged her mother and then ran into her father's waiting arms. He engulfed her in a bear hug while her mum looked on with a smile.

"What a nice surprise! You are most welcome. Come on in."

She led them into her sitting room with a beautiful wide grin on her face. "Or am I still sleeping? Is this a dream?" she asked, wide-eyed, as they sat down.

"No, sweetheart, it is real. We are truly here in Ibafo to see you."

"Ah, it is so nice to see you both. You are looking good; I'm sure Father has been taking good care of you. Father, how have you been too? I hope you have not been stressing yourself of late?" said Funmi.

"So how have you been my daughter? Have you been well lately?" Mrs Adebire asked, staring intensely at Funmi's eyes, and touching her to see if she would react to any form of pain.

Funmi knew better than to hide anything from those searching eyes.

"I have been down for some time but I'm okay now. Mum, you need not be alarmed. I said I'm okay now. Don't you trust me?" said Funmi

"Er, I do, dear. It is just that your father and I have been a bit worried about you and now to hear that you have been down confirms our worries all the while said Mrs Adebire. Yes, our sixth sense must have been in overdrive, affirmed Mr Adebire.

"How have you been coping?' Mrs Adebire queried. What has your mother-in-law been up to these days? Has she not stopped her nagging yet?"

She has not stopped, but Dotun has been helping so far. I don't blame her She said.

"Let me get you some drinks and snacks while I make lunch. You are sure not going back today I hope?" she begged.

"Sorry dear, we must. But we'll leave later in the evening, just to spend some time with you.

"Ah, and I was thinking of having you two all to myself for the weekend. Anyway, I'm glad you came." She said.

She ran off to get drinks and snacks. "She looked a bit peaky to me." Mrs Adebire commented as soon as Funmi was out of earshot.

"Now, my dear, don't start that. She looks fine, she only needs to rest." Said Mr Adebire

"Well, I still think she is not fine but since she says she is, we would have no choice but to believe her" she submitted.

Funmi returned with the drinks and snacks and served them.

She gave her father his usual smoothie.

My daughter, sit down and let's talk. You see as regards your mother-in-law's nagging, don't allow it to get to you. Although the energy exuding from her is not what you need , but I must tell you she is just being human, albeit insensitive. God will give you and Dotun your own children at His own appointed time. You just need to calm down and trust His timing. All things work together for good if we put our trust in God. Very soon, this house will be filled with a lot of people wining and dining for your child's naming ceremony. He encouraged.

"Omo mi, my jewel. It is well with you, I wasn't barren. Therefore, you will not be barren. The Lord will answer your hidden prayers. Your Father and I have not ceased in our supplications to God to intervene in your matter. All will be well; thank God you have an understanding husband. That should make you joyful." She encouraged. "Thank you so much dad and mum for the prayers. I am so grateful," said Funmi.

Let's fast and pray for a week. I believe God will show us some revelation and help strengthen and uplift our souls. Mrs Adebire said.

Inform your husband about it immediately. Mr Adebire instructed.

I will do just that Sir, so can we start tomorrow? Funmi asked.

Tomorrow would have been a good time to start but

considering that your mum and I did not plan to stay for more than some hours today and that both of you would need to create room for this fasting by properly transmitting and delegating responsibilities to your various employees, I think we should start on Monday. When we start, no one would go out. "We will all be indoors praying and seeking God's face, "Mrs Adebire said.

The trio settled down to a pleasant exchange followed by a delicious lunch of amala and ewedu. Soon it was time to part and what a moving scene it was. There was the usual exchange of hugs and a few errant tears from the two women.

The following week, Funmi's parents came to stay with her, and her husband as agreed to wait upon the Lord for a child. They all decided not to go to their place of work for a week to have full concentration in seeking God's face for intervention.

They fasted from morning till evening and break their fast at exactly six o'clock in the evening every day. They ensured they prayed and sought for God's mercy.

Six months later, Funmi became pregnant again. Her joy knew no bounds, same for her husband and Funmi's parents. Everyone began taking care of her to avoid any miscarriage again since it took several months for her to conceive after the last miscarriage.

Fast forward to the week of her expected delivery, it was the usual monthly business meeting with her clients from abroad. Being the CEO of her business, she sat at the president's seat and took charge of the meeting. She felt pain like contractions but tried not to let it show. Gradually, the feeling became pronounced. She felt more severe pain that she could not hide it anymore. Help! Funmi screamed!

Suddenly, people ran in all directions. Luckily there was a medical personnel in their midst who took adequate control of the situation. Within a short while, they got her into the car and took her straight to her family hospital. Someone informed Dotun of his wife's condition. Dotun was quite afraid of the news because Funmi's expected date of delivery is in another 2 weeks. Immediately, Dotun rang Funmi's parents to join him at the hospital and also started to pray while he made his way to the hospital.

At the hospital, the doctor promptly embarked on getting her delivered, seeing that her water has broken, and she has dilated adequately for the baby to be born.

Dotun and Funmi's parents sat side by side in the waiting room while moving their lips in what seemed like knocking on heaven's doors in prayers.

Funmi lay on the bed in the delivery room, wriggling in pain. As she was asked by the doctor to push, she kept trying her best to do so despite being tired. After about twenty-three minutes, she was delivered of her baby boy.

The doctor and nurses were very happy. "He's a very handsome boy." One of the nurses said.

The Doctor walked down the corridor with a happy face

toward Dotun and Funmi's parents. Dotun ran towards him as soon as he saw the doctor coming.

"How far doctor," he said with a voice laden with emotion. The doctor patted him and said congratulations young man, you have a handsome boy. The nurse will bring him out shortly."

"And my wife, Sir, ere r Funmi, how is-s-ss she, my wife?" he stammered.

"She is fine. She is resting now."

"Please, doctor, can I see her, please, can I?"

Dotun followed the doctor into the ward to see his wife. She was already sleeping. He bent and planted a kiss on her forehead.

Both grandparents had drawn closer too. They were happy about the baby and thanked God for answering their prayers. Dotun met his in-laws admiring the baby. They cooed over him fondly. They stopped and turned their gaze on Dotun as he approached them.

How is she? How is Funmi?" They asked.

She is fine and resting. He carried his baby and smiled. Thank you Jesus, this is indeed miraculous.

GRACE

CHAPTER ONE

THE CRISIS

Dorcas parked her car beside the main housc, A duplex that housed the landlord and his family. She occupied a small building at the back of the duplex, but it's better than some houses at least. It was painted in the same colour as the main house - a carton colour and cream. The chalet consisted of a sitting room, a big bedroom, a kitchen, a toilet and a store. The kitchen door led to the well-kept garden. The chalet has comfortable chairs too.

Dorcas slid out of the car slowly as the car door slammed after her. She searched carefully and weakly in her bag for her bunch of keys. She extracted the bunch and opened the front door to her house.

The living room has a lovely picture of Dorcas when she graduated from university. The furnishing denoted good taste. The cream-coloured cushion chairs complemented the window and the wall too.

Dorcas threw her bag on the table, and then pulled off her shoes as she walked toward the bedroom. She gave her zipper a pull with anger and the gown fell in a pool at her feet. She wore a short and free dress.

She opened her bedside drawer and brought out a bottle of pain reliever, uncapped it, popped a tablet into her mouth, and washed it down with a glass of water. She slowly entered her bed to relax.

The pain continued to increase, so unbearable that she clenched her teeth. The pain shot through her marrows as she screamed. She felt like she would crash anytime. She got so tired of life.

"Yeh-eh! Oh-hhhhh-hh! Jesus help me. These pains and agony are too much for me to bear.

She kept weeping and sobbing uncontrollably on her bed. Within a few minutes, she was already sweating and had lost weight.

If only the pain would go. It had started subtly as she prepared for work. She had taken a mild pain-relieving drug, gone off to work as she is not lazy and ignored the aching. By the time it was getting to three o'clock in the afternoon, she had almost blown up. Pain shot through her body, and she didn't think twice before asking for permission to go home.

The HR had no option but to allow her to go home to attend to herself.

Dorcas felt the pain had subsided till it started all over again, in this case, it was from frying pan to fire. Her gown was wet and hung clumpy on her body. Pin-like pain raked her body and she burst into fresh, uncontrollable tears. It seemed as if time stood still. Arms crossed, watching as pain ravaged her marrows.

The following day, Dorcas drove into the premises of the company where she works as a sales Manager and ran upstairs to her office. She exchanged greetings with a few other staff

who politely asked about her welfare as that was the next day at work after her sickle cell crisis the previous day. She felt a bit sad and decided to move on. She loved her job and ensured she puts in her 100 percent despite her occasional health crisis.
She dropped her bag on the table. Leye, her colleague came to check up on her in her office.
Hi Leye, Dorcas called out.
"Whao, look at my damsel friend. You look very fine today, how are you? How is your health now? He sat opposite her.
"Leye, thanks a bunch for your assistance yesterday. I am very grateful." He dismissed her words with a wave of his hand and a wink on his face.
There is nothing to be grateful for. Besides, what are we friends for? I would expect you to do the same for me if the situation was the other way around.
I am fine now, moving on with my life." Dorcas winked at him.
"Are there drugs to help cure this sickle cell anaemia?" asked Leye
"I'm afraid there is none. The best is for couples to avoid getting married to a partner with a genotype that can result in the couple having children with this disease, that is, AA should marry either AA or AS or AC and not AS or AC individual getting married to another AS or AC partner. Also, other drugs help relieve the pain, Diclofenac, Folic Acid, and so on, but

they should be taken as advised by a medical practitioner. It is not worth the stress to give birth to people like me who end up living in pain. The best is for couples to let go of themselves when they have found out about their genotype before having an intimate relationship. She explained.

"That's hard but you just said the right thing, I'm glad you are back, and I have missed your troubles. It is nice to have you back." He said.

"Thanks, I am happy to be back. I was beginning to get bored at home after getting better late last night and I am tired of watching movies. She said.

"I understand you. What you should be getting now is some care, fries, chicken, and ice cream to top it." He chuckled.

Dorcas replied and said. Awwn, thank you dear friend, I can't wait to have it on my table."

Consider it done, I'll make an order and it will be delivered right away. He replied with a smile.

"Let's get back to business, the managing director will have something to discuss with you at noon today. I suggest you check your desk; some matters await your attention. Enjoy the rest of the day, don't hesitate to call me if you need my help or attention Dorcas." With that, he went quickly out of her office to attend to other things at his own office.

CHAPTER TWO

THE BREAK UP

Dorcas took a deep breath, took a final look at the sack letter she saw on her table and walked briskly down to the manager's office. She rubbed her left palm over her tired face and was almost crying. It seems the world was turning upside down before her.

The managing director's confidential secretary, Stella Badmus, looked up as she walked in. She turned her full attention to the computer, totally ignoring Dorcas as she already knows what she came for. On her part, Dorcas acted like she didn't know Stella was rude.

"Good morning Stella, how are you?"

"Morning, what can I do for you ooo?" Stella mumbled, still not looking up to attend to her.

"I'd like to see the managing director."

"I'm sorry my oga is very busy."

Stella shook her head, keeping to her earlier protest.

"Look Stella, just do me a favour to announce my presence via the intercom and let me see him or else, I'll go in unannounced," Dorcas noted with amusement as the lady's face contorted in defeat.

Stella knew she had no option but to oblige Dorcas' request. She pressed the buzzer and said, "Sir, Dorcas is here to see you."

After a short pause, with an expectation of refusal from him. The MD spoke. "Send her in," he said.

Dorcas gave her the sweetest angry look and headed towards the MD's door.

She hurriedly greeted him and showed him the sack letter she got on her table. He suddenly stopped what he was doing and lashed her with words which she would never forget in her lifetime.

"Madam, your lingering health crisis is affecting your productivity at the office, and we cannot condone this any longer. Sickness today and another issue tomorrow. The last time I checked, I employed you as the sales manager of my company. But what have I gotten in return?"

"Miss Dorcas."

"Yes Sir."

"You came into the services of this company last year, right?" He asked quickly waiting to get an answer.

"Yes Sir," Dorcas answered.

"That makes you ten months old on the job and I have been paying you salaries every month without any noticeable increase in the overall sales and turnover of the company." He stated rather than asked.

"I am sorry Sir, but I have been trying my best. Just that the economic situation is not helping matters," she said meekly.

"Madam, your illness is not an excuse for not doing your job well and you are not in the right position to blame the country for the bad economic position. please leave my office." He shouted.

No amount of Dorcas' plea could change his mind. She had no option but to pack her things and go back home to think about the next steps in her life. At the same time, she was trying not to aggravate her pain any further knowing she is just recovering.

Dorcas was in a foul mood for months. She felt mad with herself anytime she remembered the bad words her boss spoke to her. Even though it's his company, courtesy demands he bears in mind to be polite even if he was going to terminate her appointment on health grounds.

She had done her best to move on with her life but found it rather challenging and quite impossible. She kept asking herself if it was a curse to be a sufferer of sickle cell disease. She also questioned her parents' decisions to place their love for each other above the pain and depression she currently feels.

Solomon looked up from the pile of work before him as He massaged his shoulders. He looked tired due to the stress of the work.

I need to make it down to Dorcas' house. She has been ill for some time, and I have not heard from her in a while. He voiced his thoughts aloud.

Who is Dorcas to you? I have seen her around you a couple of times. Is she your sister, niece, or girlfriend, if I may ask? Tade, his assistant asked as she turned to attend to her work.

"Dorcas is my girlfriend, okay?" He smiled. Tade got the

message.

I'm sorry if I am urging too much. Just that I've heard about her often from you."

Dorcas is a godly and hardworking lady, cultured, and soft-spoken with a modest background. He respects and adores her. But contrary to his love for her, his mother and Dorcas have not been on good terms. Mrs Rhodes, Solomon's mother never likes the fact that her would-be daughter-in-law doesn't like fashion and is not an extrovert like she is.

Solomon, what is wrong with Dorcas? She is not an outspoken or extroverted type of person. I've tried several times to invite her to parties, but she has always rejected. She does complain about work and will want to go home to rest. Yeah, I know she is hardworking and well cultured but at the same time, she needs to love and enjoy life by spending time outside her work to socialize.

Mrs Rhodes had shown concern for some days as regards Dorcas' health thinking it was malaria and asked if she had seen a doctor and what the diagnosis was. Solomon had watched his mother look pale and dumb at the mention of Sickle Cell Anaemia. She quickly altered her expression when she saw Solomon's countenance.

"Interesting! It never crossed my mind, " she exclaimed. "So that beautiful girl is a Sickler? How come? But her parents are literate people, right?" She asked.

Solomon nodded as he answered, "Yes, they are. Her father is a professor, and her mother is a nurse. But what has that got to do with her being a Sickler?" Solomon asked with a raised eyebrow.

Mrs Rhodcs shrugged,"I feel with their level of education, they ought to know better not to marry and bring up children who will live in pain. Everyone knows that if both couples have sickle cell traits, they are medically incompatible."

Solomon purposely delayed telling his mum about his girlfriend's condition because he anticipated her reaction and knows she would flare up. Becoming restless, he got up and strolled around the room.

"Mother," he called. "Are you saying because of medical incompatibility, two people who are in love should not get married?" His voice, painfully low, quivered. Mrs Rhodes' voice rose in tension.

"So, what if I say so? Solomon, the medical professionals advise against couples marrying if they both have sickle cell traits that will endanger their lives and that of their children. The parents are seen to undergo perpetual emotional pains and depression as their children grow because they are often at the hospital even at odd times." She snapped. He turned to face her with a quizzical look. "Since when did common sense become a determinant factor in cases such as this?" Solomon queried, arms akimbo.

She got up and stood across her son and ready to speak in the same tone she addressed him when he was only a child. She was stern with him. "Now, listen, my boy, if you choose to be irrational about this, I will not let you off easily. I don't want a Sickler for a daughter-in-law. Have I made myself clear? I want an asset as a wife and not a liability that will stress the life out of me. If you think you will marry her then I am ready to disown you forever.

She fumed away before Solomon could find the right words to say. He knew his mum is a hard nut to crack. He knew it could come to this one day. Ever since the confrontation with his mum, he has been acting cold to Dorcas. Just then he snapped out of his thinking as soon as the alarm in his office sounded. He packed his things as he cleared the table and drove back home.

Dorcas and Bolu her friend stayed awake to help her search and apply for jobs online. Hopefully, she believed she could get one soonest.

I must force my eyes to stay awake. I need to apply for at least five jobs. I must not finish my savings before I get another job," Dorcas said, gently massaging her brow. She played one of Tope Alabi's songs. The following morning, Solomon her boyfriend called her to break up with her on phone.

Hello Solomon, how have you been? I've been trying to reach you for days, but your number has always been busy. What's up?" She brought herself to ask, making use of the opportunity.

“Nothing,” he replied slowly.

“Look Solomon, I know something is wrong, just tell me.” Her voice trembled as she spoke and her heart began to beat very fast.

"Well, err, er, actually, I'd wanted to tell you, I've been thinking of this for a long time, but I didn't want to hurt your feelings. I've been troubled greatly by our medical incompatibility. You know that I am the only child of my mother, and my mother doesn't even want us to get married. She has been against it and while I love you with all my heart, I’m afraid the thoughts of spending the future together and the thoughts of watching you suffer uncontrollable pain is not what I would be able to bear for years whose end I do not know.

Immediately, Dorcas hung up the call without waiting to hear the remaining words from him. Her feelings changed from love to hatred, tearing her apart with fury, but she cautioned herself. She cried her heart out and sobbed continuously. Thankfully, Bolu, her friend is always by her side, and she took charge of the whole situation by consoling and staying with her in the meantime.

Bolu, with all I have been through lately, I am fully ready to deliver a paper at the forthcoming Conference titled, The Sickler to the World.

"The Sickler to the World?," Bolu questioned.

"Uh-huh," Dorcas answered.

Three weeks after was the day of the conference. Dorcas as promised Bolu delivered a very great speech sharing her life experiences and statistics from research which she has carried out on Sickle cell anaemia. Her level of confidence won the hearts of many. Due to the confidence she exuded while delivering her paper she was able to get a job with Mega Growth Investment Limited. The conference lifted the spirit of sicklers who attended the program. It was also an eye-opener to advocate for people to marry compatible partners and never to get carried away with love. She also encouraged sufferers on how to cope with living with the disease. The program received wide media coverage as it was televised on major television stations in the country and streamed on several social media platforms. People from all walks of life gained from the conference.

Two years after starting her new advocacy job with Mega Growth Investment Limited, she started to notice her boss, Godspower, paying special attention to her. They have gone on several dates but never discussed anything other than their passion to educate more people about Sickle cell anaemia. On one Saturday afternoon while at home, Dorcas heard a shrill ringing of the doorbell which cuts into her thoughts. She stood up and went towards the door to see who the guest was.

"Hello," Dorcas greeted smiling at Godspower at the door. Good to see you." She was surprised to see her boss turned friend.

Godspower settled himself comfortably in his seat. He surveyed the room and silently commended Dorcas on her unique taste in furnishings as she just changed some of her fittings in her living room. He wondered if the woman in the kitchen was her mother or sister.

Godspower sipped his drink and stood up immediately after he saw the woman enter the living room.

Godspower, please meet my elder sister, Mrs Ezekiel. Sis, here is my boss, Godspower Andrew.

Immediately, they both got acquainted and shared some pleasantries.

After cooking, Dorcas set the table and the trio sat to eat lunch together. Dorcas' sister asked Godspower if he liked the lunch.

"Oh, I love it!" Godspower exclaimed. "That was delicious and sumptuous."

"Waoh! I am happy you loved the meal. It's good to have you spend some time with us.

"Godspower laughed wholeheartedly. Just then, Dorcas walked in and was surprised at the level of conversation between her sister and Godspower. Dorcas has been trying to keep Godspower at arm's length for some time because she doesn't want to be ravaged with love only to suffer heartbreak again like she did in the hands of Solomon.

She doesn't want to open her heart to any man so soon due to the failed relationship she had with Solomon due to her health condition. Understandably, Solomon broke up with her because he doesn't want to attract the wrath of his mum asides from his other comments about doing life with Dorcas in expected pain. After spending time with Dorcas and her elder sister. He took his car keys to leave for home.

"You remind me of my mother so much," he told her as he was stepping out of her living room.

"Thanks for the nice evening Dorcas. See you at the office on Monday. He said happily.

"Thanks for coming around Godspower. I appreciate the visit. She smiled and waved at him as he drove out of her compound.

A few months later, Dorcas found it impossible to ignore Godspower. She practically suppressed all thoughts of him being a lover and concentrated on her job to avoid conflict of interest, after all, he did give her a job and stayed with her during a few other crises she suffered since joining Mega Growth Investment Limited. Godspower has been very attentive and always been by her side, supporting and encouraging her during these hard times. Dorcas has been battling entertaining feelings for her boss, but she bore the acts of unrequited love, so she was not in a hurry to dive headlong into another relationship.

Godspower asked her out and still acted like a friend to her. After about two years of getting to know each other, Godspower took up the courage to propose to her.

Dorcas, you are very beautiful" he said with all sincerity.

"Thank you," she replied sheepishly.

"Will you marry me?" asked Godspower

She thought her ears played a trick on her.

"What did you say?" She questioned, cocking her right ear in his direction.

"I said, will you m-a-ar-ry me?" Godspower repeated.

She was stunned. The possibility that he would propose marriage never crossed her mind.

"Are you joking?"

She laughed hysterically. "I can't think right now. My head seems to be sniffled with cotton wool. Why do you want to marry me?" she asked, gazing intently at him.

"I want to marry you because I see you as my best partner, the woman I want to spend the rest of my life with. I want an understanding helper who'll share the applausc and passion to help others with me. I desire someone who I can proudly refer to as my wife and who will bear my future kids.

"Look Godspower, don't flatter me with words, please. Your reasons are good. But I'm sure you'll find them in a beautiful and hardworking lady who is not a Sickler like me.

I don't care about your health status. All I want is you. He affirmed.

" Please give me some time to think about it. Mmm? Be patient with me," she begged.
"Okay, no problem. I'll give you two months to think about it". He begged.
Six months after the proposal, they got married. The marriage ceremony was beautiful and colourful. Both families were proud and blessed the couple.
God blessed the new family with a bouncing baby girl. Being that Godspower is of the AA genotype, there was no concern about the little girl being a Sickler. As expected, she is AS.

CHAPTER THREE

SICKLE CELL INITIATIVE

One year later, she established Grace Health foundation, which focused on supporting anyone who has health challenges either young or old and ensuring they get free health care and those that were beyond the power of the organization got support through Dorcas' and Godspower's influence to get medical care abroad.

Dorcas and her husband were able to get international sponsors from other countries to build hospitals in their country. People around the vicinity were able to get subsidized health care because of this too.

That same year, Dorcas started an advocacy to sensitize people about Sickle Cell Anaemia. She organised various conferences and went as far as universities, colleges, and polytechnics to create more awareness among people as regards medical compatibility. She doesn't want people to undergo the pain she went through. She wants to put a stop to Sickle Cell Anaemia.

She decided to establish an initiative called "STOP SICKLE CELL INITIATIVE". She went ahead to advocate that blood group and genotype tests should be free for couples who want to know their medical compatibility. She has gone as far as reaching the remote villages in her state to sensitize people. She was also able to use her influence to establish a primary health centre there and people were able to get free medical care.

Dorcas' selfless action to humanity made her gain worldwide

attention from the nooks and crannies of the world as a person who suffered from sickle cell anaemia and decided to sensitize people not to be blind to love and cause pain for their unborn kids.

During one of Dorcas' initiative outreaches, She gave speeches and sensitized people with passion. This made everyone love her and partner with her initiative as donors and sponsors.

In her speech she said. "AS and AS partners are not medically fit and compatible to bear children without standing the risk of having a child with SS. Anyone who goes ahead to marry under the guise of love should bear in mind the risks of having SS children and the challenges these children may suffer growing up and eventually settling down to marry using her life experience as an example. She added that although she forgave her parents for taking this step to marry despite knowing their genotypes, other children may not forgive such acts, especially with the increasing knowledge available today as offered by organisations such as the Stop Sickle cell initiative. In her words, she said to parents, "don't bring children to the world to suffer from a disease with no medication . "You don't want to spend days at health facilities, times in depression and spend all your earnings to take care of them and sometimes watch them die as not all of them live to marriageable age.

When she was giving her speech, she felt uncomfortable with herself. She couldn't take it anymore and rounded up on time. She felt it within her that her time has come. She was glad she has sensitized the society for a decade and a half and done well for humanity. She was rushed to the hospital and her family doctor was able to give her quick and utmost attention.

But she knew the clock is ticking for her to go back home. She decided to talk with her husband. She needed to do the needful before giving up the ghost.

She said slowly. "My husband, thank you so much for being my Godsent from above. During my crisis and troubles, you stood by me. If it is within my power, I'll add extra years to my life, but it seems the end has finally come. Please take good care of Deborah, our only child and I pray that the Lord will be with you both." She gave up the ghost at the age of forty-two. It was a trying time for Godspower, but he decided to move on with his life as he knew her time was up, and she needed to rest. She had gone through a lot.

Dorcas' death moved her fans and people to tears. Godspower decided to hand over the Stop Sickle Cell Initiative to Dorcas' assistant who has stood strongly behind her since the commencement of the initiative. Her story became the talk of the own. Godspower's happiest moment afterwards was that Dorcas' life and situation impacted a lot of people to say no to medical incompatibility.

In the fifth year after Dorcas died, Godspower was invited to deliver a keynote address at the conference where Dorcas met Godspower. He titled the address “Grace” and in his words, he mentioned Dorcas as a child of grace who impacted the world around her for the forty-two years she lived. Everyone in attendance could not hold back their applause to celebrate Dorcas more and donations worth several millions of dollars were received to build an ultra-modern hospital to cater specially for people living with sickle cell anaemia. The hospital was named Dorcas- child of Grace Hospital.

What an impactful life Dorcas lived.

ABOUT THE AUTHOR

Remilekun Jaiyeola is a poet, life coach and master storyteller, an art he developed growing up as a voracious reader. He is passionate about telling stories to people of all ages, steering up change in the hearts of his readers. He believes "stories leave us with memories" when we teach children, coach teens, train adults or sell products and services

He studied Biochemistry at the University of Ilorin and worked with a tier 1 commercial bank for about 14 years before proceeding to study Digital and Strategic Marketing at the University of Bradford, UK. He is also an alumnus of emLyon Business school France where he studied Advanced Strategy and Branding.

He is husband to Dayo and father to 3 excellent children. He loves to relax by listening to music, especially Jazz.

www.ingramcontent.com/pod-product-compliance
Lightning Source LLC
LaVergne TN
LVHW052057160826
845678LV00015B/3274
* 9 7 9 8 3 5 2 2 8 6 8 9 0 *